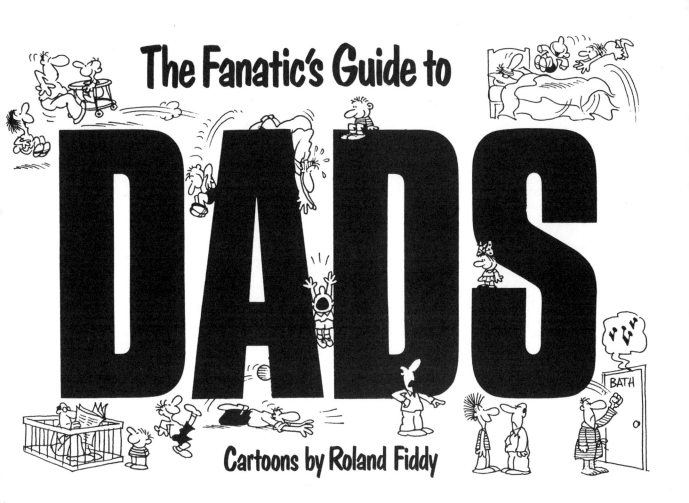

The Fanatic's Guide to DADS

Cartoons by Roland Fiddy

In the same series:
The Fanatic's Guide to Cats
The Fanatic's Guide to Computers
The Fanatic's Guide to Diets
The Fanatic's Guide to Dogs
The Fanatic's Guide to Golf
The Fanatic's Guide to Men
The Fanatic's Guide to Money
The Fanatic's Guide to Sex

First published in the USA in 1992 by Exley Giftbooks
487 East Main Street, Suite 326, Mt. Kisco, NY 10549-0110.
First published in Great Britain in 1990 by
Exley Publications Ltd, 16 Chalk Hill,
Watford, Herts WD1 4BN, United Kingdom.

Second and third printings, 1991
Fourth printing, 1992

ISBN 1-85015-246-2

A copy of the CIP data is available from the British Library on
request.

Typeset by Brush Off Studios, St Albans, Herts AL3 4PH.
Printed and bound in Hungary.

Roland Fiddy

Roland Fiddy, Cartoonist.

Born in Plymouth, Devon. Studied art at Plymouth and Bristol Colleges of Art. Works as a freelance cartoonist and illustrator. His cartoons have been published in Britain, the United States, and many other countries. Has taken part in International Cartoon Festivals since 1984, and has won the following awards.

1984 Special Prize, Yomiuri Shimbun, Tokyo.

1984 First Prize, Beringen International Cartoon Exhibition, Belgium

1984 Prize of the Public, Netherlands Cartoon Festival.

1985 First Prize, Netherlands Cartoon Festival

1985 "Silver Hat" (Second Prize) Knokke-Heist International Cartoon Festival, Belgium.

1986 First Prize, Beringen International Cartoon Exhibition, Belgium

1986 First Prize, Netherlands Cartoon Festival

1986 First Prize, Sofia Cartoon Exhibition, Bulgaria.

1987 Second Prize, World Cartoon Gallery, Skopje, Yugoslavia.

1987 "Casino Prize" Knokke-Heist International Cartoon Festival, Belgium

1987 UNESCO Prize, Gabrovo International Cartoon Biennial, Bulgaria.

1987 First Prize, Piracicaba International Humour Exhibition, Brazil.

1988 "Golden Date" award, International Salon of Humour, Bordighera, Italy.

1988 Second Prize, Berol Cartoon Awards, London, England.

1989 E.E.C. Prize, European Cartoon Exhibition, Kruishoutem, Belgium.

1989 Press Prize, Gabrovo International Cartoon Biennial, Bulgaria.

1990 First Prize, Knokke-Heist International Cartoon Festival, Belgium.

1991 Prize for Excellence, Yomiuri Shimbun, Tokyo.

Becoming a father for the first time can be traumatic.

Nowadays, childbirth is often a shared experience.

However, that is only the beginning ...

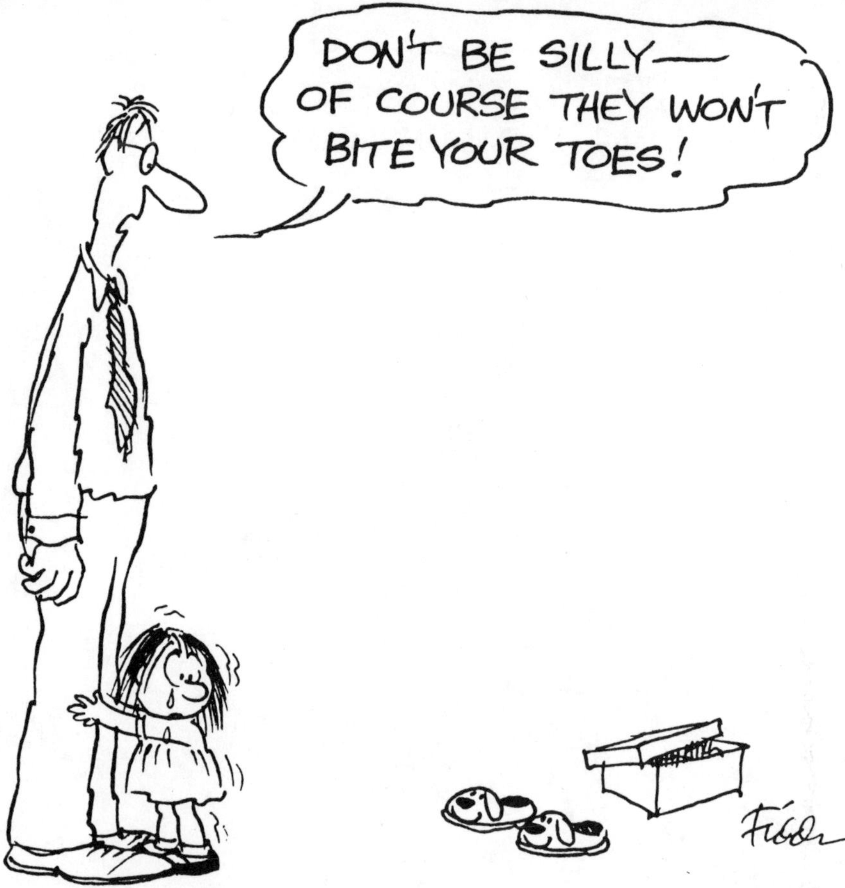
DON'T BE SILLY—
OF COURSE THEY WON'T
BITE YOUR TOES!

Suddenly they seem quite grown up ...

I'M HEARTBROKEN! DAVE IS TAKING OUT ANOTHER GIRL!
1
BUT YESTERDAY YOU SAID YOU DIDN'T LIKE DAVE— YOU WERE GOING TO TELL HIM YOU DIDN'T WANT TO SEE HIM ANY MORE!
2

The 'Fanatics' series £2.99 (paperback)

The **Fanatic's Guides** are perfect presents for everyone with a hobby that has got out of hand.... Cartoons by Roland Fiddy.

The Fanatic's Guide to Cats

A must for cat lovers everywhere who cannot fail to find fun and laughter in the frolics of our feline friends.

The Fanatic's Guide to Diets

Sixty percent of women are either on a diet – or breaking a diet. Men are surprisingly fanatical too. This is Roland Fiddy's sympathetic laugh at life for the majority of us who keep popping out at the waist.

The Fanatic's Guide to Golf

This is the one gift that the golfer will love.

The Fanatic's Guide to Money

Money makes the world go around – this hilarious book will appeal to the haves and have-nots alike.

The Fanatic's Guide to Sex

Now this is one that you won't give to Aunt Matilda – unless she's really liberated! On the other hand, your lover, your husband or wife, your (selected) friends and some of your family will find it hilarious and in moderately good taste....

The Crazy World series £3.99 (hardback).

There are now 18 different titles in this best-selling cartoon series – one of them must be right for a friend of yours....

The Crazy World of Birdwatching (Peter Rigby)
The Crazy World of Cats (Bill Stott)
The Crazy World of Cricket (Bill Stott)
The Crazy World of Gardening (Bill Stott)
The Crazy World of Golf (Mike Scott)
The Crazy World of the Handyman
   (Roland Fiddy)
The Crazy World of Hospitals (Bill Stott)
The Crazy World of Jogging (David Pye)
The Crazy World of Love (Roland Fiddy)
The Crazy World of Marriage (Bill Stott)
The Crazy World of Music (Bill Stott)
The Crazy World of the Office (Bill Stott)
The Crazy World of Photography (Bill Stott)
The Crazy World of Rugby (Bill Stott)
The Crazy World of Sailing (Peter Rigby)
The Crazy World of the School (Bill Stott)
The Crazy World of Sex (David Pye)
The Crazy World of Skiing
   (Craig Peterson & Jerry Emerson)
The Crazy World of Tennis (Peter Rigby)

Great Britain: Order these super books from your local bookseller or from Exley Publications Ltd, 16 Chalk Hill, Watford, Herts WD1 4BN. (Please send £1.50 to cover post and packing on 1 book, £2.25 on 2 or more books.) Exley Publications reserves the right to show new retail prices on books which may vary from those previously advertised.